LOVELY FRANCE

A Relaxing And Stress Relieving Coloring Book For Adults

CAFÉ PARIS

FRENCH HACKING

Contents

Contents

TABLE OF CONTENTS

French Hacking was created to teach French students how to learn the language in the shortest time possible. With hacks, tips & tricks we want our students to become conversational and confident by teaching what's necessary without having to learn all the finer details that don't make much of a difference or aren't used in the real world. Check out our other books by searching French Hacking on Amazon!

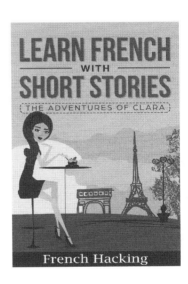

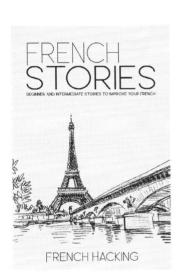

If you enjoy the book or learn something new, it really helps out small publishers like French Hacking if you could leave a quick review so others in the community can also find the books!

1. Eiffel Tower

The Eiffel tower, is a Parisian landmark that is also a technological masterpiece in building-construction history. When the French government was organizing the International Exposition of 1889 to celebrate the centenary of the French Revolution, a competition was held for designs for a suitable monument. More than 100 plans were submitted, and the Centennial Committee accepted that of the noted bridge engineer, Gustave Eiffel. Eiffel's concept of a 300-meter (984-foot) tower built almost entirely of open-lattice wrought iron aroused amazement, skepticism, and no little opposition on aesthetic grounds. When completed, the tower served as the entrance gateway to the exposition.

Fact: The Tower was only meant to stand for twenty years, but when over two million people came to visit the structure and the city of Paris during the World's Fair of 1889, the people's view began to change.

2. Louvre

Louvre, also known in full as "Louvre Museum" or "French Musée du Louvre," is the national museum and art gallery of France, housed in part of a large palace in Paris that was built on the right-bank site of the 12th-century fortress of Philip Augustus. It is the world's most-visited art museum, with a collection that spans work from ancient civilizations to the mid-19th century.

Fact: The Louvre is the biggest museum in the world. It is so big that it will take about 100 days to do a complete tour and cover each of the paintings. Touring the whole museum in just one day is next to impossible.

3. Palace de Versailles

Listed for the past thirty years as a UNESCO World Heritage Site, the Palace of Versailles, in French "Château de Versailles," constitutes one of the finest achievements of French art of the 17th century. The former hunting lodge of Louis XIII was transformed and extended by his son Louis XIV who installed here the Court and the government of France in 1682. Up until the French Revolution, a line of kings succeeded each other, each taking his turn to embellish the Palace. The Hall of Mirrors, the King's Grand Apartments and the gardens make the Palace of Versailles one of the most visited cultural sites in the world today.

Fact: The Hall of Mirrors within the palace has a total of 357 mirrors.

4. Côte d'Azur

The Côte d'Azur, also known as "French Riviera," refers to the beautiful Mediterranean coastline which stretches along the southeast corner of France. Though having no official boundary, most people consider it to range from the Cassis commune in the west, all the way over to the town of Menton which lies upon the French-Italian border. The main city of the French Riviera is Nice, known as the queen of the Riviera. Other places include Monaco (with Monte-Carlo), Cagnes-sur-Mer, Antibes (with Juan-les-Pins), Cannes and St. Tropez.

Fact: The Côte d'Azur benefits from up to 330 days of annual sunshine, seventy one miles (115 kilometers) of coastline, eighteen golf courses, fourteen ski resorts and 3,000 restaurants.

5. Mont Saint-Michel

Mont-Saint-Michel is a rocky islet and famous sanctuary in Manche département, Normandy région, France, off the coast of Normandy. It lies forty one miles (sixty six kilometers) north of Rennes and thirty two miles (fifty two km) east of Saint-Malo. Around its base are medieval walls and towers above which rise the clustered buildings of the village with the ancient abbey crowning the mount. One of the more popular tourist attractions in France, Mont-Saint-Michel was designated a UNESCO World Heritage site in 1979.

Fact: Second only to Santiago de Compostela in Spain, Mont-Saint Michel was an important pilgrimage of faith during the Middle Ages. Such was the difficulty of the journey that it became a test of penitence, sacrifice, and commitment to God to reach the Benedictine abbey.

6. Loire Valley Châteaux

The Châteaux of the Loire Valley, known in French as "Châteaux de la Loire," are part of the architectural heritage of the historic towns of Amboise, Angers, Blois, Chinon, Montsoreau, Nantes, Orléans, Saumur, and Tours along the Loire River in France. They illustrate Renaissance ideals of design in France. The châteaux of the Loire Valley number over three hundred, ranging from practical fortified castles from the 10th century to splendid residences built half a millennium later. When the French kings began constructing their huge châteaux in the Loire Valley, the nobility, drawn to the seat of power, followed suit, attracting the finest architects and landscape designers. The châteaux and their surrounding gardens are cultural monuments which stunningly embody the ideals of the Renaissance and Enlightenment.

Fact: Many of the smaller chateaux are still lived in by the actual owners. Chateau de Brissac is the tallest chateau in France and has been in the same family since 1502. 514 years later, descendants of the Marquis and Marquise still live in the chateau with their children.

7. Cathédrale Notre-Dame

The Cathedral of Notre-Dame de Paris, a masterpiece of Gothic architecture, is one of the most visited monuments in France. It was built in the Middle Ages, at the far end of the Île de la Cité. Work started in the 13th century and finished in the 15th century. Badly damaged during the French Revolution, the cathedral was restored in the 19th century by the architect Viollet-le-Duc. Its many visitors come to admire its stained glass and rose windows, the towers, the steeple, and the gargoyles. They can also discover the Notre-Dame treasury and have a go at climbing the towers to enjoy a panoramic view of Paris.

Fact: The Notre-Dame organ involves almost 8,000 pipes (some dating back to the 18th century) played with five keyboards, making it the biggest pipe organ in France.

8. Provence

Provence is a geographical region and historical province of southeastern France, which extends from the left bank of the lower Rhône to the west to the Italian border to the east, and is bordered by the Mediterranean Sea to the south. It largely corresponds with the modern administrative region of Provence-Alpes-Côte d'Azur and includes the departments of Var, Bouches-du-Rhône, Alpes-de-Haute-Provence, as well as parts of Alpes-Maritimes and Vaucluse. The largest city of the region is Marseille.

Fact: Provence is renowned for being the largest rosé-producing area in the world. Around 88% of wines made in this region are rosé! It's pale pink color and elegant flavors are their signature.

9. Chamonix-Mont-Blanc

Chamonix-Mont-Blanc, more commonly known as Chamonix, is a commune in the Haute-Savoie department in the Auvergne-Rhône-Alpes region in south-eastern France. It was the site of the first Winter Olympics in 1924. Situated to the north of Mont Blanc, between the peaks of the Aiguilles Rouges and the notable Aiguille du Midi, Chamonix is one of the oldest ski resorts in France. The Chamonix commune is popular with skiers and mountain enthusiasts, and via the cable car lift to the Aiguille du Midi, it is possible to access the off-piste (backcountry) ski run of the Vallée Blanche.

Fact: The legendary Marathon du Mont Blanc has been run since 1979 and is growing exponentially. In 2019, 10,500 participants participated.

10. Alsace Villages

Alsace is a cultural and historical region in eastern France, on the west bank of the upper Rhine next to Germany and Switzerland. The region is famous for its wine, its colorful half-timbered houses, the richness of its gastronomy, and its castles which sit enthroned on the summits of the Vosges mountains. Alsace is also one of the more fertile regions in central Europe. The hills are generally richly wooded, chiefly with fir, beech, and oak.

Fact: Alsace has changed hands between France and Germany many times in the past. The overall characteristics of the architecture, infrastructure, economy and interests generally point towards a more Germanic outlook than French.

11. Carcassonne

Carcassonne is a French fortified city in the department of Aude, in the region of Occitanie. It has a population of about 50,000 and it's located in the plain of the Aude between historic trade routes, linking the Atlantic to the Mediterranean Sea and the Massif Central to the Pyrénées. Its citadel, known as the Cité de Carcassonne, is a medieval fortress dating back to the Gallo-Roman period and was restored by the theorist and architect Eugène Viollet-le-Duc in 1853. It was added to the UNESCO list of World Heritage Sites in 1997.

Fact: The first signs of settlement in this region have been dated to about 3500 B.C., during the Neolithic time.

12. Rocamadour

Rocamadour is a village located in the Occitanie région, in southwestern France. Its buildings, overlooked by a 14th-century château, rise in stages above the gorge of the Alzou River. The village owes its origin, according to tradition, to St. Amadour (or Amateur), who chose the spot as a hermitage. It became a place of pilgrimage in the early Middle Ages. More than 200 steps lead up the rock to the sanctuary. The churches in the sanctuary include the Romanesque basilica of Saint-Sauveur and the 12th-century crypt of St. Amadour. The lower town consists of a long street with fortified gateways and a restored 15th-century hall.

Fact: The sanctuary of the Blessed Virgin Mary within the village has attracted pilgrims from many countries for centuries, among them kings, bishops, and nobles.

13. Château de Chenonceau

It's a French château spanning the River Cher, near the small village of Chenonceaux in the Indre-et-Loire département of the Loire Valley in France. It is one of the best-known châteaux of the Loire Valley. The estate of Chenonceau is first mentioned in writing in the 11th century. The current château was built in 1514–1522 on the foundations of an old mill and was later extended to span the river. The bridge over the river was built (1556-1559) to designs by the French Renaissance architect Philibert de l'Orme, and the gallery on the bridge, built from 1570–1576, to designs by Jean Bullant.

Fact: Chateau de Chenonceau had seen a lot during two major wars (WWI and WWII), however, the largest degree of damage was done during the 1940 Cher River flooding. A young agronomist Bernard Voisin was in charge of a complete Chateau's restoration starting in 1951 and was able to bring life back to the Palace and its adjacent lands.

14. Vieux Lyon

Lyon Old Town is a Renaissance district at the foot of the Fourvière Hill. With its paved old streets, colorful façades and secret passageways (les Traboules), the Vieux-Lyon was a key element in getting the city listed as a World Heritage Site by Unesco.

Fact: The Traboules are hidden passageways that have witnessed many secret happenings in the past. There are said to be 400 traboules concealed between various buildings within the town. First created in the 4th century, Traboules have been used by locals, silk weavers, and most recently, the French Resistance, who used them to hide from the Gestapo.

15. Promenade des Anglais

Promenade des Anglais (Walkway of the English) in Nice is the most important attraction in the city. It stretches for four miles (seven kilometers) and provides an uninterrupted view of the azure sea and palm trees. Its name comes from the English aristocrats who came to Nice in the 18th century to enjoy the health benefits of the local climate. At that time, the shoreline was not so regular, and because the lords and their wives wanted to walk comfortably, a seaside promenade was built (with the hands and finances of the English people).

Fact: Among the English aristocrats that passed by the Promenade des Anglais, other prominent figures included Queen Victoria and Winston Churchill.

16. Étretat

To the north west of France lies Normandy, a region well known for its natural beauty, culinary perfection and history. Along its northern coastline is the small town of Étretat, a very picturesque place that has gained immense popularity among tourists as it still retains its old historical culture, giving all visitors the small town cozy feeling. Étretat is famous for its exceptionally characterful and majestic cliffs, known as les falaises d'Etretat. Sculpted by the waters of the English Channel, the cliffs of Amont, Aval, and the Needle (L'Aiguille) form an enchanting setting that raise up to 300 feet (ninety one meters) high.

Fact: Trou à l'homme (meaning "manhole") is a tunnel dug through the Aval cliff which connects two beaches. What makes it special is that it is only accessible for a few hours a day, at low tide.

17. Deauville

Deauville is a commune in the Calvados département in the Normandy region in northwestern France. With its race course, harbour, international film festival, marinas, conference center, villas, Grand Casino, and sumptuous hotels, Deauville is regarded as the "queen of the Norman beaches" and one of the most prestigious seaside resorts in all of France. As the closest seaside resort to Paris, the city and its region of the Côte Fleurie (Flowery Coast) has long been home to French high society's seaside houses and is often referred to as the Parisian riviera.

Fact: In France, Deauville is known perhaps above all for its role in Marcel Proust's novel, "In Search of Lost Time."

18. La Seine

Possibly the world's most famous river, the Seine not only captures our imaginations in the present day: it has mesmerized and seduced those who encounter it since pre-medieval times. Neatly dividing the city of Paris into distinctive left and right banks (rive gauche and rive droite), the river has served as a source of sustenance, commerce, and breathtaking perspectives since a Celtic tribe of fishermen known as the "Parisii" decided to settle between its banks, on the tiny strip of land today referred to as the "Ile de La Cité," in the 3rd century B.C. The river runs for 482 miles (776 kilometers) through France and into the English Channel at Le Havre and Honfleur. Its source is in the French region of Burgundy, and its mouth is the English Channel.

Fact: In Paris, the banks of the Seine are connected by a total of thirty seven bridges, including the "Pont de l'Alma" near the Eiffel Tower, the "Pont des Arts," and the "Pont Neuf."

19. Café Procope

Café Procope is the oldest and among the most famous Parisian restaurant/cafés. It was the original European "Literary Café" prototype. Located in the 6th arrondissement on Paris' Left Bank, and steps from Boulevard Saint-Germain, it retains its former glory and original charm. This café's rich backstory represents an enormous part of the socio-cultural history of café culture in Paris. Inaugurated in 1686 by Italian Francesco Procopio dei Coltelli, it did not take long for it to develop something of a reputation for being the meeting spot for intellectuals and coteries of distinguished people.

Fact: French philosopher and satirist Voltaire's favorite table serves as a kind of shrine at the Procope, decorated with candelabras and tomes of the author's work. The marble table appears to have suffered a bit of damage, but honors the name of the eighteenth-century writer and Encyclopedist.

20. Lourdes

Nestled in the foothills of the Pyrenees Mountains, Lourdes is France's most important Catholic pilgrimage site. Millions of visitors come to Lourdes every year for spiritual inspiration. Some arrive to bathe in the waters in hopes of miracle cures. To the faithful, Lourdes is known for the seventy validated miracles that have occurred here. The main pilgrimage sites, the Grotto (where Saint Bernadette received her divine visions), and the Basilique du Rosaire are surrounded by a serene woodland alongside a tranquil babbling brook. Marian processions take place every evening at nine p.m. from April through to October. The procession of hundreds of pilgrims holding candles is a breathtaking sight to behold.

Fact: Although Lourdes has a population of around 15,000 inhabitants, it is able to take in some 5,000,000 pilgrims and tourists every season. The town has the second greatest number of hotels in France after Paris with about 270 establishments.

21. Toulouse

Steeped in history dating back to the 13th century, Toulouse is known as "The Pink City" because of its distinctive red-brick architecture. These buildings reflect the sunlight in a rosy-toned hue. While ambling the pleasant town squares and basking on outdoor café terraces in Toulouse, visitors soak up the laid-back vibe of this beautiful and balmy city. The UNESCO-listed Canal du Midi runs through Toulouse and flows all the way to the Mediterranean port of Sète near Marseille. The tree-shaded path along the canal is popular for leisurely strolls and cycling.

Fact: As the headquarters for Airbus, an Airbus guided tour is the landmark tourist activity in the city.

22. Saint-Émilion

Saint-Émilion is a charming medieval village located in the heart of the famous Bordeaux wine area. It is a very unique site where world-famous wineries, fine wine, beautiful architecture, and great monuments are a perfect match. Legend has it that the town bears the name of a Breton monk that performed miracles while living an exemplary life. In order to retire from social life, he settled in a natural grotto in 750 A.D., which can still be visited nowadays in the heart of the town. Saint-Émilion has a long history of being a commercial and prosperous village, as well as a trading center of all the goods produced within the area (wines, grains, stones, etc.). It was also a renowned pilgrimage site, and boasts the relics of the local patron saint; the town was quite prosperous in the Middle Ages, which is reflected by its emblematic monuments such as the underground monolithic church.

Fact: In 1999, for the first time in the world, a vineyard was written on the World Heritage List by the UNESCO as a Cultural Landscape, that is to say a historical landscape that remained intact but which is still carrying on its activity.

23. Nimes

Famous for its ancient cultural heritage and the warm southern sun, the city of Nimes appears untouched by the passing of time. The place has some of the most preserved Roman monuments in continental Europe. Its historical center has a charming ancient atmosphere with lots of tree-lined streets and fountain-decorated public squares. In addition to the appeal, outdoor cafes submerge Nimes' cobblestone pedestrian neighborhoods.

Fact: The Nimes Amphitheater has a seating capacity of 24,000, and even though it is not the most imposing by size, it is among the best-preserved Roman amphitheaters still standing today.

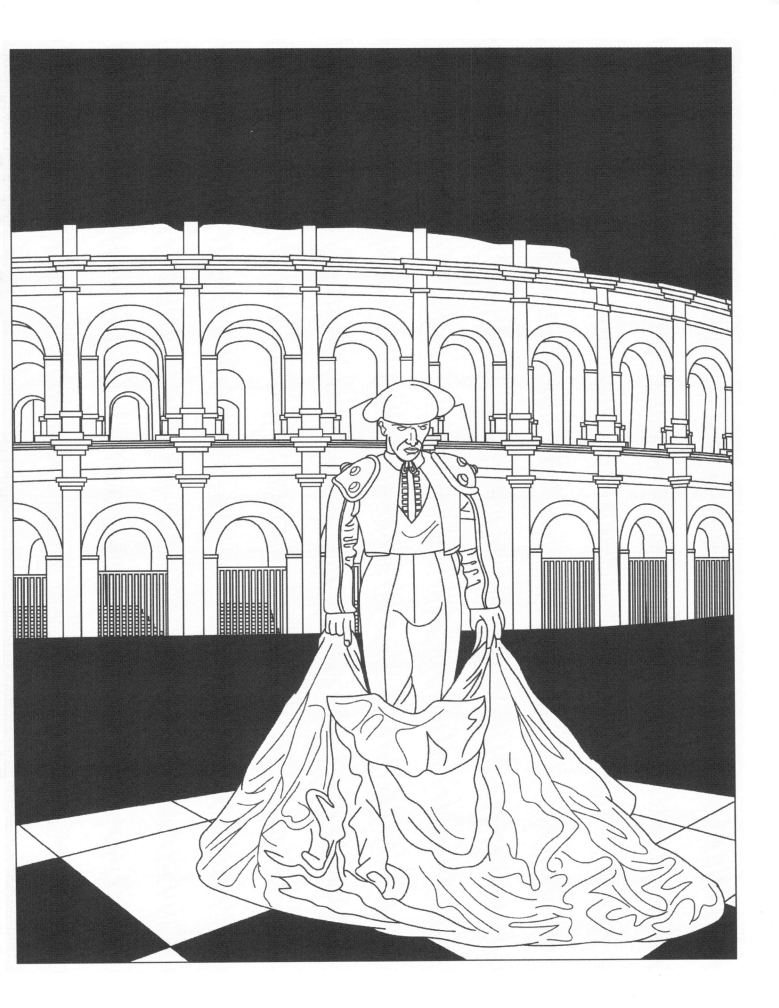

Made in the USA
Columbia, SC
13 April 2021